Your Amazing Itty Bitty™ Guide to Parenting Like a Leader

15 Universal Shifts to Raising The Stand-Out Adults of Tomorrow

Janet Krebs

Published by Itty Bitty™ Publishing
A subsidiary of S & P Productions, Inc.

Copyright © 2025 Janet Krebs

All rights reserved. No part of this book may be reproduced or transmitted in any form or by any means, electronic or mechanical, including photocopying, recording, or by any information storage and retrieval system, without written permission of the publisher, except for the inclusion of brief quotations in a review.

Printed in the United States of America

Itty Bitty™ Publishing
311 Main Street, Suite D
El Segundo, CA 90245
(310) 640-8885

ISBN: 978-0-9992211-5-0

This book is for educational purposes only. Nothing should be taken as medical or mental health advice, diagnosis or treatment. Always check with your doctor before changing your diet, altering your sleep habits or starting a new fitness routine.

What Does it Mean to be a Parent?

Here are 15 universal shifts to raising the stand-out adults of tomorrow!

Parenting requires a unique blend of leadership, dedication, and patience to nurture your child's growth, health, and success throughout their lives. Your task is monumental: raise a child to become a thoughtful, kind, successful, and independent adult.

In her book, *Your Amazing Itty Bitty™ Guide to Parenting Like a Leader,* Janet Krebs provides strategies that inspire you to become a successful leader in your personal environment.

In this book you'll discover how to:

- Become a leader in your everyday life
- Communicate effectively
- Prioritize your family without guilt
- Empower kids to make decisions and solve problems
- Build a legacy you can be proud of
- And much more…

If you're ready to become the parent you've always aspired to be, pick up a copy of this must-read Itty Bitty™ book today!

Dedication

Dear Benjamin and Elisa,

When I look at each of you, I see dreams, hope and promise.

When I speak with each of you, I hear wisdom, insight, and determination.

Thank you both for being the indelible smile printed on my heart.

Remember: Think Socks!

Stop by our Itty Bitty™ website to find interesting blog entries regarding Leadership Parenting

www.IttyBittyPublishing.com

Or visit Janet Krebs at

JanetKrebs.com

Table of Contents

Introduction
Shift 1. Get Ready for a Parentshift!™
Shift 2. Keep Family First Without Apology
Shift 3. Create Connection and Legacy
Shift 4. Identify Your Values and Live Them
Shift 5. Make Family Members Seen and Heard in Your Home
Shift 6. Communication: More Than Words
Shift 7. Say Yes to Self-Care
Shift 8. The Unwelcome Guest is Electronic
Shift 9. The Household Economy is a Game Changer
Shift 10. Be a Boss, Not Bossy
Shift 11. PS and DM: Not What You Think
Shift 12. Failure Is a Necessary Option
Shift 13. The Important ABCs
Shift 14. Responsibility is a Great Teacher
Shift 15. To be or Not to be a Parent

Introduction

Why are there pages of instructions with your new coffee maker, yet you leave the hospital with a newborn human and no owner's manual?

Your job is fundamental: shape and prepare your child to be an independent adult: one who is able to leave home and live in society. Sounds simple enough, doesn't it?

Are you kidding? This is daunting as hell. Twenty-plus years of uncertainty, guessing, trial and error, tears and laughter, frustration, and joy.

My Ben and Elisa are flown and grown adults. They inspired the writing of this book, along with the thousands of kids I influenced over the years.

Within these pages, you'll find information that will posture you as the leader you are, and help you undertake the challenge of raising the stand-out adults of tomorrow.

Shift 1
Get Ready for Parentshift!™

Parenting is leadership and YOU are getting a promotion! It's time to elevate parents to the executive status they deserve. Parenting requires a dynamic combination of leadership skills to support children's growth, health, and success throughout their lives.

When you recognize leadership qualities like influence, vision, communication, and collaboration, it is easy to see how they overlap.

Within these pages, parent(s) will be loosely defined or referenced as adults with influence over young people. If you are still reading, this is written for you or someone you know!

1. Leaders organize people toward common goals. You do this daily, monthly, and annually! Think mornings or bedtime.
2. Leaders inspire others to believe in a plan and work toward the desired result. (Yes, getting to school or graduating on time can be inserted here.)
3. Effective leaders affect change. This includes actions, behaviors, or outcomes. How many times have you changed routines or bad habits?

Feel the Parentshift™ to Leadership

Let's talk about who leaders are and what they look like. Look through these descriptions. You're sure to see yourself.

- Great leaders work for a shared vision.
- Leadership is a posture, not a position.
- Leaders work long and hard like you do every day!

These characteristics sound selfless and thankless yet don't confuse this with being a pushover. Leaders simply serve the common cause. Leaders are seen as:

- Team players
- Flexible
- Effective Communicators
- Having a great attitude
- Willing and able to make hard decisions

Remember, leadership is everywhere. Keep reading to see and identify yourself as a leader. Step into it. The Parentshift™ has begun!

Shift 2
Keep Family First Without Apology

Have you ever learned a lesson the hard way? As a working mom, keeping family first without apology was one of those moments for me. I suspect every working mom has felt this struggle.

Leaving a sick child at home is a key example. You have overwhelming guilt and distraction. Remember that your tombstone will name you as a mother, daughter, wife, but never banker, teacher, mail clerk, etc. Be the parent, and embrace your emotions without apology.

Expect this as reality. You may feel conflicted and it can be hard at times. Accept this going in; be proud of this role.

1. As a parent, priorities shift. Your paid job is important, but not above family.
2. Thinking you can block out your home life when working and believing they won't collide is a trap.
3. Whenever possible, choose a professional environment that values family. Remind and encourage your kids to do the same as they get older and make their own career decisions.

What You Need to Shout From the Rooftop!

Home and family are foundational. They are central to your life. Home and family ground you as the primary source of connection. They set the tone for almost everything else.

- You can't perform optimally in life when your home life is off-balance. It is hard, if not impossible, to focus when one foot is walking into work while the other is replaying any morning drama.
- Be present. Be intentional with your actions. Some things can't be undone.
- Family is your "why," the purpose that drives you to do most things.

Leaders model behaviors that others respect. What can you model that is worth replicating?

- Remember to acknowledge your loved ones especially when you leave and return home, and make them feel special.
- Be someone people like to be near and spend time with.
- Adopt the shift and be the leader who proudly puts family first, and influences others to do the same without apology. This is where change will start.

Shift 3
Create Connection and Legacy

Connection is key! Connection is feeling joined in a relationship. Kids must feel and know that they belong to someone, somewhere, and that they matter. This is integral to success. When connections are anchored in love and trust, everything else builds solidly and securely.

1. Connection is simple and costs nothing.
2. Be intentional and creative.
3. Make connecting a habit and a priority. It will be part of your legacy.
4. Connections are made when you are assertive and strict as long as it's done with love.

Here are some starter ideas in case you wonder "how to begin?"

1. Hold a family meeting. Plan casual time to come together and check in.
2. Plan intentional time to organize a meal, play a game, walk, or any other healthy activity.
3. Allow your bedtime routines to have room for talking, storytelling, or daydreaming.

Make Breaking Bread a Priority

Mealtime is a natural time to connect. I am a fan of daily family dinners, but four times a week is more realistic with today's families going in dozens of different directions.

- Plan for intentional conversation. Start with open-ended questions. "Tell me about your day" is inviting. "How was your day?" invites a single-word answer like 'good' or 'fine' and does little to promote meaningful conversation.
- Share the highs and lows of the day during dinner. It requires a bit of thought and invites storytelling. This time is magical and never gets old as the kids get older.
- When your kids are young, pack a lunch napkin with a special note or simply kissed with fresh lipstick. For just a moment during their day, you connect with them.
- I was known to take a small bite of my kid's sandwich. (Yep, they remember.)

There is no substitute for building connections, and there is no right or wrong way. Create your own fun ways to connect. When a hose is not hooked up, there is no water. If a lamp is not plugged in there is no light. Connection matters. Point made.

Shift 4
Identify Your Values and Live Them

This discussion is foundational to building a strong family. Take a minute and think about this!

1. Values are individual principles or standards that motivate people to act one way or another.
2. Values guide human behavior.
3. Core values define your character.

When was the last time you thought about and identified your values? How do you model and communicate them to others? Can the people in your life articulate and describe your values?

1. Knowing your values affects how you do things. How you do anything is how you do everything.
2. When actions and behaviors are inconsistent, it's an indicator of weak or nonexistent values.
3. Values are personal. Keeping them at the top of your mind will help guide you. Take a moment now and jot down some ideas about your own values.

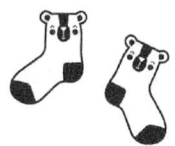

Values Change as You Change!

Values change throughout life as you mature, gain experience and change roles. The values you had in your 20s, were likely influenced by your family. As years and experience accumulate, you adopt values that align with your changing self!

What do the people in your life know without a doubt that you value? Can they tell by your actions, patterns, focus, and attention? For some of you, this will be simple and very obvious. Others may be transitioning to a different time in life and your values are changing. Here are some common human values:

- Lifelong learning
- Prioritizing family
- Being Integrous
- Being true to self
- Acting with intention
- Spirituality
- Honesty
- Gratitude

You'll find you gravitate toward people who share values that are similar to yours.

Action item: Reflect on this for yourself: what do you want your family to see in you? What are your legacy values? Write them down.

Shift 5
Make Family Members Seen and Heard in Your Home

You are the Chief Parenting Officer (CPO) of your home. Say it out loud right now. "I am the Chief Parenting Officer in my home!" You are the leader, the one, the adult your kids look to for guidance and direction. They are looking to you as a role model.

1. If there are two of you who share the parenting work together you are very lucky.
2. Work toward creating a clear vision for the whole family as well as for each individual.

Being seen and heard in your family is where children learn what being valued feels like. It is essential for developing a positive and confident self-view.

1. This will require habitual presence, intention, and attention.
2. Allow room for curiosity, to listen and learn from your young people.
3. Remember, their world is different, thus creating a new perspective you need and should want to know about.

Why and How Do You Do This?

Being seen and heard leads to healthy mental and emotional behaviors. Maintain the objective of raising the successful, healthy adults of tomorrow. You can make mistakes and still do it right the first time.

Being valued promotes the following:

- Having the confidence to speak up and ask for what you need.
- Learning to stick up for yourself builds healthy relationships in the arenas of work, school, home, friendship and love.
- Opening yourself up to creative and innovative thinking in all areas. All ideas matter!
- Developing leadership by listening and respecting the opinions of others.

This is obviously a *CliffsNotes* start to everything that can be said on this subject. You are invited to continue your own list and regularly audit this concept in your home.

Ask your kids if they feel seen, heard, and valued at home. Then be prepared to listen and adjust as needed. This will be very insightful, and you may get unexpected answers. So, take a breath and go for it. You will be so glad you did. If you need help, contact me at ask@janetkrebs.com

Shift 6
Communication: More Than Words

There are volumes written and researched about communication, and for good reason. What you say, when you say, and how you say things have caused much pain, passion, and promise throughout time. Here is a framework to help you begin improving your own communication skills.

If you understand and practice the principles in Shift 5, your communication style becomes equally important.

1. Are you a skilled, patient, and interested listener, ready and engaged to learn more during a discussion?
2. Are you the nagging, bossy, or over-communicator type, not allowing space for anyone else's voice?
3. Does your body language communicate active listening?
4. Can you craft one magical question to give any conversation momentum?
5. Can you be a present and genuinely interested listener? Everything is not always about you.
   (Ouch! Sorry, not sorry.)

Meaningful vs. Trite Subject Matter

You cannot build meaningful relationships without listening and understanding. The best way to accomplish this is through shared experiences and shared conversations.

- Be aware of your **tone** of voice.
- Do you speak **at** people or **with** them?
- Do you ask more open-ended questions?
- Are you willing to share personal stories, be vulnerable, and human?
- Be observant of body language: uncross your arms and maintain eye contact.

Communication skills have always been a big deal for me. As a life-long educator and subject facilitator, speaking is my tool, and effective speech was a priority at home. Here are two tips that proved fun and effective:

- Make **good** and **fine** forbidden words. Remind kids they are developing a better command of vocabulary rather than relying on two neutral, nondescript words. "Tell me about your day?" will get you a colorful answer.
- Encourage speech contests and other opportunities to speak in public. Your kids may hate it, yet they learn how to eliminate fear, speak with confidence, make a point, and speak on stage. **Yes, they will thank you later.**

Shift 7
Say Yes to Self-Care

As a parent leader, it is your privilege and responsibility, to care for others. Self-care is especially important and no, it is *not* selfish. Get over that thought right now. If you're not feeling great, you can't be of service to others.

1. Today's holistic health care includes and endorses mind, body, and spirit. Nurture all whenever possible without guilt.
2. Plan for it, but keep it simple. Adding a chore to your already-hectic schedule feels hard and therefore difficult to sustain.
3. Publicize your habits, your thoughts, your why, and the benefits. This allows you to set an example instead of telling others what to do. Your kids are always looking to see what you are doing.
4. Make sure to keep your communication positive and avoid using blaming language. "You are driving me nuts so, I need to take a walk," is different from, "I am feeling stressed; I will be a better mom after I take a walk." #**parentshift**

What Does This Look Like for the Family?

You may receive resistance, so be prepared to step up as the leader.

- Self-care includes good nutrition for all. You can put limits on what is consumed and when. Close the kitchen after it's been cleaned, and lunches are packed. Fruit is a handy snack option requiring no cleanup.
- Oreos were purchased only twice a year. Boy did the kids learn how to make them last vs. scarfing them all in one day!
- Complaining about boredom is never your responsibility. Encourage activities like reading, or learning; literally anything but electronics. If they still complain, they can clean their rooms or clean the house.
- Kicking the kids out of the house is a viable option for your sanity. Every prior generation has survived and thrived from outdoor play.
- You can encourage family walks, games, park visits, or outings. Any change of scenery is great.
- Music is a creative way to inspire people. Change the mood throughout the house with music and see what happens.
- Remember, giving yourself a break teaches others to do the same. *WIN*!

Shift 8
The Unwelcome Guest is Electronic

We have all reconciled, embraced, and adapted to a world dependent on electronics. I have yet to meet anyone who doesn't have a strong opinion about the role of electronics. They are here to stay, so your job is to integrate them responsibly into your life and the lives of your children. The keyword here is **"responsibly!"**

42% of kids have a phone by age 10. Over 90% of all kids have a phone by age 14.

Yes, times have certainly changed. You will face this decision at some point. This includes decisions about social media accounts, security apps, and rules around usage. Know your position and be firm yet know when to re-evaluate and pivot as well

Remember:

1. Firm parental leadership matters.
2. Assess each child at their individual stage.
3. Your child's voice matters. Hear them out. Their ideas may impress you.

How to Tame the Electronic Monster

This is a perfect opportunity to visit the question of *why*. It's a fun place to start the discussion, as it invites thoughtful reasoning from your child.

- "Because all my friends have one," is never a good enough answer.
- Your child may tell you a phone makes them feel connected and safe. This helps you understand how important security is to them.
- When you say yes, create agreements up front. All parties need to understand the consequences when the privilege is misused or abused.
- You will quickly understand the powerful leverage the phone gives you as long as you are paying for it.
- No phones allowed in the bedroom.
- Reserve the right to change your mind. If your gut tells you something is off, listen and pull the phone. If you say no, and later reconsider, be prepared to enjoy exaggerated sloppy affection.
- Age does not accurately indicate readiness.

Your leadership and ability to firmly uphold your agreements will determine the success of this arrangement.

Shift 9
The Household Economy is a Game Changer

Money. Value. Budget. Expenses. Allowance. The money conversation is important, and no, it has nothing to do with your income. This shift will change so much in your family.

1. Today's kids are assaulted by consumer influences, choices, and pressures related to having the latest and the greatest. I call it comparisonitis. It's criminal, really.
2. Kids use "stuff" as peer pressure and competition, potentially leading to bad feelings. Kids can be very mean.

So, what can you do? How can you avoid being the bad guy in purchasing decisions? I am so glad you asked. The household economy is your secret weapon. Here is an example:

"Mom, can I have $20.00 to see a movie?"

"Gosh, I am so sorry. Your account is low. You haven't made a deposit in a while"

1. Eye rolling begins.
2. Negotiation gears are turning.

After the Eye Rolling ...

"Well, what can I do around here to make a deposit in my account?"

I kid you not, this was the actual conversation. No negotiating, whining, or meltdown. They knew I was the manager of the money account. They also knew I was reasonable, and once they contributed or made a deposit, it was an easier yes.

I had the cleanest grout in town. Even a four-year-old can use a grout eraser. (Yes, it's a thing.)

This is not a question of what you *can* afford, it's about what you *want* to afford. No apologies.

Justifying $120 shoes for growing feet is hard. Once your price is established, your child can pay/work off the rest or make a different decision.

- This builds values and pride of ownership, since they have skin in the game.
- Your kids can check their account balance before making a request. You are never the bad guy, just the gatekeeper.
- This shapes their own consumer values. Sometimes they may skip a purchase that they decide "isn't worth it."
- Being responsible for their own spending power enables your child to deflect any peer pressure they may have experienced.

Shift 10
Be a Boss, Not Bossy

I waited until now to make you a boss, just in case you needed a little fire in your soul to own it. Don't worry, you've got this whole Parentshift™ concept. This is *you* standing empowered, confident, and curious to get started as the leader in your home. Let's do this!

The following are privileges and responsibilities to be respected by **all** family members:

1. You set the tone of the household.
2. You are the role model, and everyone is watching you very carefully.

Don't be the memorable bad boss witch in *The Wizard of Oz,* who didn't even have a name!

1. Fear and intimidation do *not* work when you are motivating and influencing.
2. Help others avoid feeling helpless, out of control, and without choices.
3. "My way or the highway" simply doesn't work.
4. The Wicked Witch of the West mostly had monkeys working for her. That should tell you something

Parenting Is Leadership

You have young people in your home and/or in your circle of influence. That means you are a leader, a role model, an influencer.

- What vision do you have for your kids?
- Do you accept that one of your primary jobs is to foster confidence and a strong sense of self?
- Do you understand that you are raising an adult who, eventually will step out and be successful on their own?
- Do you understand that building his/her strong wings to leave the nest means you did your job really well?

You want to lead those who are:

- On time, and good time managers
- Willing to help get things done
- Good communicators
- Able to ask questions and ask for help
- Emotionally mature
- Excellent listeners
- Self-starters
- Kind and team players

This is a short list to get you started on your own. As the leader in your home, what is your vision and what strategies will you create to reach your vision?

Shift 11
PS and DM: Not What You Think

Problem Solving and Decision Making.

I suspect you were thinking **p**ostscripts and **d**irect **m**essages.

Did you know that an average human makes no fewer than 25,000 decisions a day? Of course, this takes into consideration factors like age and level of responsibility.

1. As you mature, your decisions go from minor and routine to complex and impactful.
2. Problem solving and decision making are learned skills and must be practiced.

Imagine being a child for a moment. There is a beautiful apple that you really want on a table just beyond your reach. Would you think through all these possibilities?

1. Pull over a chair to stand on.
2. You cry and wait for help to come.
3. Grab the step stool.
4. You choose a different snack.
5. You abandon the idea altogether.

Many Years Later ...

You are a tween/teen with a dilemma: two social invitations conflict with each other. You also promised to have dinner with your favorite grandma, who is recovering from minor surgery.

This is quite a dilemma. Are you equipped and experienced in breaking down choices? How do you weigh your options and ultimately decide on a course of action? Do you reach for outside opinions or decide for yourself?

- Your kids need practice doing this, so they can experience the frustration and the confidence that comes from standing by their decision.
- Conversely, if you jump in and rescue throughout those integral practice years, you rob your youth of learning the necessary skills to help them succeed.

Imagine all the life opportunities to practice DM and PS between the apple and the invitation scenarios. What to wear, eat, read, play, and learn, to name a few. One day it will be a decision about college or a job transfer, another drink at the bar, how to choose where to live, or the person you want to share your life with.

A parent's job is to coach and encourage the *practice* and *process* so that kids can thrive with confidence on their own!

Shift 12
Failure is a Necessary Option

You first heard, "Failure is not an option," during the tremendous popularity of the film *Apollo 13*. Outside the space program, I am declaring that failure is crucial for personal growth and development. It is 100% critical and necessary.

1. Failure builds resilience, which is key to your ability to survive. Accepting challenges, disappointment, and bouncing back is critical.
2. Making mistakes permits you to let go of perfectionism. This is where major growth occurs.
3. Humility is an attractive trait to nurture, a quiet partner for failure.

You learn this as a baby first learning to walk. Each fall is celebrated, and you are enthusiastically encouraged to keep trying. *When does the shift away from this occur?* This same encouragement and support needs to relentlessly carry over into your parenting. Inspire your kids to step out and try new activities, hobbies, classes, or sports. Persist even when they resist. They will thank you later, trust me.

A Moment to Reflect

It's natural to look back and question some of your parenting decisions. You do the best you can at any given moment. Some decisions make you feel solid, and some may make you shake your head.

- In life there are winners, and there are *learners*. Often at the same time.
- While you set your kids up to succeed, they must try something new even if it's scary. This is a perfect life-skills opportunity to push their comfort levels.

There is strategy in choosing activities that allow kids to practice taking risks. This develops grit and personal accountability. Allow your kids to sit in both joy and disappointment. During these moments inviting reflection and understanding is *golden!*

It's important to understand that failure is not a reflection of self-worth or competence. It is about trying, stretching, and growing. It is most important they learn to try again or try something different. But get up and try again, they must.

As the adult, what is your relationship with failure? Make sure you project a healthy perspective to your children. They need permission to learn and grow resiliently.

Shift 13
The Important ABCs

Accountability, **B**oundaries, and **C**onsequences! These are the most important nouns, concepts, practices, ideas, and rules you will continually bump up against. When you get comfortable with them and integrate them into your home, life will get easier. I stand by this bold promise.

This discussion is an introduction at best. The entire book could be written on just these imperative ABCs. Please allow this chapter to spark curiosity to explore further.

1. **A**ccountability is accepting responsibility for one's own actions.
2. **B**oundaries are the limits, guidelines, and rules that are in place.
3. **C**onsequences are the effect, result, or outcome of something.

Each of them is necessary and when they play out together, they are oh so powerful! Think about the game of life and your home as the learning laboratory where all these concepts can safely occur and be practiced. These ABCs offer order and expectations: a framework to work within.

Best Illustrated in Story

Think about the many scenarios where valuable lessons are learned. I bet they all illustrate a combination of the ABCs.

- Your kid stayed up late, missed the school bus, forgot lunch, and missed the first period exam. So, they went hungry, received an F, but never slept through the alarm the rest of the year.
- Your child negotiates a later curfew, misses it, and accepts an earlier curfew until he earns the chance to try again.
- A closed bathroom door requires a courtesy knock before entering.
- If you get caught driving too fast you get a ticket.

You'll get really good at labeling the different parts in almost every circumstance. Choosing weekend activities, spending money, and eating too much junk, offer cause and effect. It is a formula of "if this, then that." No lecture is needed when your boundaries are clearly established.

This is how the world works every minute of every day. When the ABCs are clear, life has less turmoil.

Shift 14
Responsibility is a Great Teacher

Responsibility means *you can be counted on, answerable for something, and you accept the results of your actions.* In other words, step up, do the right thing, and be accountable. Being responsible within your family breeds trust, and ignites confidence and independence for everyone.

In order to teach your children responsibility, you must give them opportunities to be responsible. If this scares you, I get it. This is a test for you as much as a test for the kids.

1. Chores are often a good starting point at any age. Even a young child can take his dinner plate to the sink.
2. As your child gets older, the level of responsibility is adjusted accordingly. Bedtime routines and homework completed independently are great benchmarks.
3. Remember, this requires consistent practice of new habits and behaviors. Expect mistakes and hiccups.

Responsibility: Something we Model

Responsibility is best taught by modeling. We raise children to be responsible people by being responsible ourselves. Reminder: Young people are always watching.

Here are some examples:

- Are you on time in life?
- Do your kids see you model organization and planning?
- Can they count on you when you promise to do something or be somewhere?
- Are you prone to making excuses?
- Do you apologize easily when you make a mistake?

As your children get older and become more independent, they will understand and appreciate the guidance and the lessons you allowed them to learn. They may not be able to articulate these feelings, yet as they grow more competent and confident living their own lives, they may come to realize the influence you had on them.

You will look at them proudly, knowing they are independent and responsible adults that you helped shape. Who they become is an important part of your legacy and the gift they will pass on to their own children and generations beyond.

Shift 15
To be or Not to be a Parent

A current measure for family readiness is to picture your life ten years into the future. If you can see yourself running to soccer, dance, or any of those parental tasks and it feels solid, you may be ready for parenthood. If not, think twice.

1. This is a great visualization to think seriously about this big decision.
2. Historically, having kids was something most people just did. It was expected.
3. Allowing this to be an option will serve young couples well.

This is a big shift. The consciousness and level of intention for kids born in the 90s is elevated.

1. Your child's global world view causes them to think about the bigger picture.
2. They feel more empowered to make decisions that may go against the norm.
3. Their scope of choices allows them to dream big, which should be encouraged.

Parenting Is a Full-Time Investment

You decide to have a baby, yet in doing so you are also deciding to *raise an adult*. This will be your full-time job until they leave the nest and live on their own. And even then, you still get to be in their lives as a parent until the day you die.

What happens in the middle is what counts the most.

- Yes, you will make mistakes.
- Yes, you will experience sleepless nights, worry, frustration, and yes, some tears.
- You will also experience unparalleled love and joy.
- You will experience pride, and understand the true meaning of unconditional.

Remember, you are a human being doing a *big* thing.

- Allow yourself to be human.
- Be the leader in your home. Step into the parent role you said yes to when you made this decision.
- Accept the mistakes along the way.
- Find humility and practice it often.

Above all, ask for help when you need it. You will be glad you did. We all have an investment in tomorrow. *Let's raise tomorrow together.*

You've finished. Before you go ...

Post/share that you finished this book.

Please star rate this book.

Reviews are solid gold to writers. Please take a few minutes to give us some itty bitty feedback.

ABOUT THE AUTHOR

Janet Krebs is your go-to speaker and leadership strategist when you need a playful heart and authenticity combined with a no-nonsense insight. With over 30 years in education and facilitation, she inspires individuals to reach and attain their maximum potential.

Janet helps parents adopt a leadership mind shift empowering them to cultivate confidence and self-reliance in themselves and their children. Her primary creative learning laboratory is the family home.

Her talks highlight leadership and parents as leaders. Janet playfully teaches audiences to embrace a Parentshift™ to effectively raise tomorrow's stand-out adults.

Janet enjoyed a rich career in consulting, human resources, and education. As Commander Krebs in a space flight simulator, she taught and influenced over 65,000 students. Her credentials include degrees in human development, counseling psychology, and K-adult education.

When asked about her greatest accomplishment, she offers a wide smile and without hesitation names her son Benjamin and daughter Elisa.

If you enjoyed this Itty Bitty™ book you might also like…

- **Your Amazing Itty Bitty™ Communicating with Your Teenager Book** – Christine Alisa, M.S.

- **Your Amazing Itty Bitty™ Family Leadership Book** – Jacqueline T. D. Huynh

- **Your Amazing Itty Bitty™ Video Gaming Addiction Book** – Sean Bryan

- **Your Amazing Itty Bitty™ Keep Your Children Safe Book** – Lynda J. Bergh Herring

- **Your Amazing Itty Bitty™ Empty-Nesters Survival Handbook** – Dr. Dorine Kramer

Or any of the many Amazing Itty Bitty™ books available online at www.ittybittypublishing.com

www.ingramcontent.com/pod-product-compliance
Lightning Source LLC
Chambersburg PA
CBHW061305040426
42444CB00010B/2535